heaven is a place
where colours
have no name

between the named and the felt

andré pb

Cover design and interior layout by andre pb
First eBook edition, 2025

Published by andre pb

ISBN 978-0-6482057-9-1

The poems in this collection were refined in collaboration
with an AI language model – a collaboration that reflects a
larger reality: whether or not we are prepared for it, the
presence of AI in our lives – and in every form of art – is no
longer a question of if, but how. We are entering a time in
which human imagination and machine intelligence are not in
conflict, but in conversation.

I believe AI will become one of the great evolutionary forces
in poetry, music, visual art – and in forms of expression not
yet conceived. As for what art may become in fifty years from
now – I cannot begin to imagine its shape. But I sense it will
be something neither of us could bring into being alone.

what survives 45

longing's threads...46

even your silence has ancestors 47

a puzzle with no frame 50

salt does not mourn 52

neither black, nor white 54

the lie that sees me 55

flicker beneath 57

the shape of pleasure 59

the hollow deal 60

carved from the dark...62

where no one dwells 63

above the path...65

when it arrives 67

hunger for hunger 69

a breath of eternity 71

no diagrams for wind 74

the last warmth...75

breath of mist 77

threads of the whole..78

CONTENTS

velvet cage ....

before you break...

doesn't take much...

when the thread is love..

walking differently ....

grace unveiled...

the wall that walks with me ....

the quiet tether...

to know how to rain ....

the gesture that carries the wind....................................

out of reach...

what light remembers ....

nothing left to bruise..

the poem I didn't mean to write......................................

the wound..

the currents of time ....

words that waited ....

let me hear the sky you carry 80

a crown of forgetting...82

colours have no name 85

velvet cage

they gave the moon
a private mirror:
now it weeps
in its own reflection.

the soul
crawls deeper
into a velvet cage
called *mine.*

before you break

it's lighter than the space
that holds nothing—
not even a shade of air.

it has no colour,
no shape—
like invisible ink
spilled on a cotton bloom,
struggling to take a breath.

it carries the weight
of the universe—
before light was born,
before motion
had a name,
nor a thought
that could drift away.

the weight of the fear
runs through the cracks,
growing like cancer—
hidden in the soul
of a dam
that will break.
but you don't know—
when,
or how.

this is what breaks you—
before
you break.

a single drop of rain
may tilt the weight—
not with intent,
just reaching
to quench thirst.
or a breeze,
meant only
to caress aching hair.

the breath always walks
on an obsidian blade.
even a whisper,
the softest plea,
can tilt the world—
held together
by nothing
but a matrix
of fragile air.

doesn't take much

it doesn't take much
to make
   someone
      happy.

   someone
who has been deprived
    of even a
       glimpse
       of love.

   someone
who's been hungry
    for days
     that melted into
       years.

   someone
who's known
    only
       one thing—
     pain.

   someone
scarred
    by injustice,
bruised
    by hate.

someone
who's never stepped
    beyond the bars
    of a cage
        they never built.

someone
who waits,
    still waits,
        for
        a word called
        freedom.

so—
why don't we give it?

when the thread is love

not all pain
is loud—

some walk in softly,
barefoot through the bones,
and settle
in the space
where a heartbeat once opened
for someone who never came.

you learn early
not to ask for too much—
just enough to breathe
without becoming
a burden.

some wounds
have no names,
only seasons
they return in—
a certain rain,
a closing door,
a kindness
you almost touched.

loneliness
is not always
being alone.

sometimes
it's speaking
and hearing yourself
echo
back
with no hand
reaching through the silence.

sometimes
it's growing older
without ever
being truly
held.

you are not wrong
for wanting
to be touched
without earning it.

not every ache
is a sign
of weakness.

some come
from carrying
what should've been
offered.

and love—
real love—
is not something
you chase.

it is
what stays
when everything
you've failed to be
is still allowed
to rest.

you are not broken
for needing
what you never received.

the heart doesn't bruise
because it is flawed.
it bruises
because it remembers
how soft
it was meant
to be.

so if you feel
too much—
that means
the thread
is still love.

and if you can,
be the hand
that does not let go,
even if
it's only your own.

walking differently

we all fall.
we all walk.

they say—
you have to fall
before you learn
how to walk.

some people
need to fall
more than others.

some people
learn
how to walk better
every time
they fall—
and they're not afraid
of falling again.

some people
think
falling and walking
are the same thing.

some people
get comfortable
with falling.

some people
believe in falling
more than
in walking.

some people
think
they
only know
how to walk.

some people
think
they walk
better
than others.

some people
resent
falling
so much
they pretend
they're walking
at all times—
even
while they sleep.

some people
are so afraid of falling,
they never
walk.

some people
only walk
with a walking stick,
or have someone
always
holds their hand—
everywhere.

some people
walk in circles,
thinking
they're moving forward.

some people
walk in dreams—
but wake up limping.

but why do we all
walk
differently?

grace unveiled

angels don't have wings—
they sprint,
as if the earth remembers
they were once stars.

they race toward you
with a heart so light
it carries galaxies—
made of nothing
but joy so pure
it stirs the sky.

they don't recall
your wrong turns,
your heavy hours.
they teach you grace
never near
the scent of wrong.

not clouds,
not mist—
you can hold them:
warm thunder,
wrapped in breath, and fur,
scented with something
older than rain.

they wait
like stones wait for sun—
forever,
without asking.

they feel you
like a second heartbeat—
quiet.
true.

where did they come from?
what strange kindness
dreamed this creature—
guiding us back
to the garden
we thought we'd lost?

angels don't speak.
they don't sing.
they only bark
when silence
asks for a voice.

the wall that walks with me

they say an accent
is like cologne from another planet—
makes you exotic,
adds flavour where there was only flour,
makes people lean in
like they're trying to hear your soul,
through a foggy radio.

apparently,
it gives you that international spice.
you become the paprika of conversation.
women get curious.
men nod with envy.
strangers assume you speak five languages—
even if you just know
how to mispronounce three
or froth
with great confidence.
sometimes,
I just conjugate the word "maybe" in five tenses and hope
for the best.

they say it makes you
mysterious, charming—
the kind of person who writes poetry in cafés,
probably barefoot,
with a tragic past involving rain,
a dog that understood you,
and the scent of burnt cinnamon.
bonus points if you also play the accordion.
badly.

and carry a notebook full of unfinished goodbyes,
dog-eared on the page that still smells like regret.

but not in my case.

in my case,
it's like walking into every room
with a goat on a leash—
people notice,
but not for the reasons you hope.
the goat also has an accent.
worse than mine.
she eats vowels.

my accent doesn't seduce.
it startles.
it's like tripping on a word
and faceplanting into a sentence.
even when I say "hello",
someone's already squinting,
like I just cursed
at their grandmother
in morse code.
long pause.
confused blinking.
silent judgment.

I've been single so long
I sometimes flirt with houseplants.
even they seem unsure.
one leaned away recently,
like it sensed I wasn't emotionally available.
another keeps texting me "new pot, who dis?"

and if someone does respond—
they're usually
a recruiter selling "the opportunity of a lifetime,"
or someone who calls me interesting
in the same tone people use
to describe a spider
inside a salad.

I make people feel things.
mostly concern.
mild nausea.
existential dread.

my circle of friends?
also immigrants.
we don't really hang out—
we just sit around
sharing the same facial expression people make
when buffering videos freeze
at 2 seconds.
we're not bonding—
we're loading.
if you listen closely,
you can hear us buffering in five languages.
our support group is just a shared wi-fi password.
we meet every time someone loses signal.

the truth is,
I trip over my accent
everywhere—
not just sidewalks,
but in phone calls,

job interviews,
first dates,
and dreams
when I try to order coffee
and end up married
to a goat named Destiny.
her horoscope said
we are a perfect match.
mine said "seek help."
the barista officiated.
the espresso machine cried.
I said "I do", and Destiny said "Maaaybe."

even when I'm silent,
my accent shows up
like a background character
with way too much screen time.
it's not just sound—
it's a feature.
a wall that walks with me,
waves at people behind me,
then quickly kicks me in the knee.
sometimes it whispers "don't mess this up"
just before I definitely mess this up.
it also narrated my failures in audiobook format,
chapter one: "Oops you did it again."

I'm tired of always falling over
nothing visible.
of getting up
with metaphors stuck to my elbows.
of putting on band-aids
that look poetic

but don't fix a thing.
of being late
to moments I rehearsed
in my head for years.
of writing replies in my mind
that always arrive
three years too late.
and still start with "dear sir or madam…" in Comic Sans.

people say,
"Just be confident."
as if confidence is Windex,
and my accent is a smudged window
that just needs
a motivational speech.

but no matter how many "you got this" podcasts I listen to,
the wall stays.
you can't paint it red.
you can't hang a sign:
"Caution: identity may shift during conversation."
you can't bulldoze it
with TED Talks and green smoothies.
believe me, I've tried.
now I just have expensive pee.

even when I learn
the difference between three and tree,
someone still laughs—
like I told a joke on accident.
and maybe I did.
maybe I am.
I'm a walking typo with charm.

a glitch with good intentions.

still, I keep walking.
even if the GPS says:
"In 500 meters, doubt yourself again."
"In 1 kilometre, repeat childhood in a different accent."
at destination: pretend it was all part of the plan.

and if I ever make it to heaven,
they'll ask about the bruises.
and I'll shrug,
smile crookedly,
and say:

the wall that walks with me.

the quiet tether

when the noise
became lightless,
you let it narrow
to breath
and a gaze
made of velvet weight—
a creature of love,
but not of your kind.

two eyes,
small,
but older than the noise—
quiet lanterns
lit by something
the world's forgotten—
holding you—
as if you are the only truth
worth remembering.
a silence
that doesn't ask you to rise,
only to stay,
and be forgiven.

you are not alone.
but the silence changes.
it drifts like smoke
into a language
you can no longer pronounce—
not absence,
but the kind of silence
that knows your name

before you speak it.

outside,
the world unknots
its voices
without you.
you watch
as your name
peels from rooms
like old paint from a gate.

and still,
this quiet tether—
a heartbeat folded into another—
holds you
like snowfall
that never touches the ground.

you are not vanished.
you just live
in the room
you've disappeared into—
gently,
as if the world
has been a dream
you've mistaken
for home.

to know how to rain

you don't give love
by feeling it.
you give it
by knowing
how to love.

what is the use of a cloud
if it never breaks?
what is the point of water
if it won't run
to reach
the root?

nothing will grow
by watching a cloud
that only watches you.

the seed remains buried
if the river
won't kiss its sleep.

if you don't know how to rain,
go
to the land
that no longer waits.

you need to walk
beside the steps
that pave the path
for you
to walk.

you need to catch
the falling leaf
before it forgets the tree.

you need to read
what's written
in the eye.
some mouths
stay closed—
but the eye
never does.

you need to hold
the hand
that feeds you
light.

you need
to give
what is yours—
not borrowed,
not spared.

you need
to give
what is
a part of you—
the part
that doesn't return
once given.

the gesture that carries the wind

no one noticed
when the pebble leaned
to let the root pass.

a finger of light folded
through a broken pane—
not to heal,
only to remain.

we are not here
to chalk outlines around grief,
or count kindness
like coins
falling through hushlight.

we are
the breath between
a moth's wing and the dark—
the moment it chooses
not to tremble.

you don't owe
the wind your thanks
for touching your hair.
but it does.

the universe
doesn't bow
to be praised
for letting rivers
remember their names.

we are not here
to measure what we give
or why.

we are here
to place a hand
on a stone
without asking
if it remembers touch.

to whisper light
into a stranger's ache,
without needing to know
what was lost.

to lift
the next second
for someone,
as if time were
a fallen leaf.

what moves the world
is not justice,
nor reason,
nor faith—
but the unseen hands
that tuck a loose thread
back into the weave,
never needing
to be known
as hands.

out of reach

can you step
beyond
your boundaries?
can you imagine
what refuses to be imagined?

can you touch
what doesn't exist
until it's touched?

who built the lock?
who forged the key?

is there a river
wide enough
to wash this longing clean?

is there a light
that doesn't travel—
just appears,
unbidden,
in the dark?

is there a pattern
that forms
all patterns
or is pattern
just another wall
we've mistaken
as a door?

I keep asking
as if asking itself
weren't the veil.

what light remembers

at times
light curves—
as if retracing
the outline
of something
it once touched.

sometimes
it reflects—
not for you
to grasp,
but to pass on—
depending
on the shade
you've chosen
to wear.

sometimes
it sinks
to the deepest part—
depending
on the clarity
of the ocean
you keep.

and sometimes
it dissolves
shadow
from shadow—
depending
on how deeply

you vanish
into its gaze.

if you still can,
learn the slow arts—
smoothing,
softening,
clearing,
unlearning—
to shape
the light that has
passed
through you.

nothing left to bruise

a fulfilled life
leaves no bruise
on a single breath—
not even
the fragile gasp
of a sparrow
in the wind.

what outlives love?
not time.
not the aching script
of memory.

before you name it—
it blooms already
in the quiet—
between the fall of dust
and the hush
of your name.

even now,
it waits
like a childhood scent
in a room
long emptied—
everywhere,
and nowhere
but you.

unfold the shape
the mirror carved.
lay down
your armour of needing.

fade—
like a vow
in silence
inside
someone's last dream.

be—
as flame is,
before it knows
it's burning.

the poem I didn't mean to write

I wrote a poem
without wanting to—
the way salt finds the sea
even after forgetting its thirst.

it was a night
quiet as unlit stars,
when the mind stepped aside
and the heart
walked barefoot
into itself.

no intention,
no elegance,
just the ink
responding to something
older than thought.

my fingers moved
as if memory had a pulse—
not the kind that recalls
but the kind that
knows
before knowing.

each word
was not chosen
but born—
not crafted
but allowed.

what touched the page
wasn't refined,
wasn't meant to be—
it was
what remains
when the flame
burns past the wick
and the air itself
starts speaking.

for months,
I forgot it.
loose pages,
silent as closed wings,
buried in time.

tonight, I found them.
and they found me back.

and I saw
what had been written
without my will,
without polish,
without fear.

it was the rawest
thing I've ever touched—
as if my own veins
had spilled
and turned to syllables.

not poetry,
not prose,
not even a cry—
but a language
too honest
to be named.

it may be
the most beautiful
I've ever written,
because I didn't write it—
I only became
the path
the feeling took
from a galaxy
to hand.

the wound

there is no one
without a wound.

we all
need to be healed.

the more we heal,
the lighter we become.

only love
is the healer.

everyone deserves
to be loved.
everyone deserves
to love.

I deserve
to be loved.
I deserve
to love.

I deserve—
to heal.

I need to let go
of the pain
and suffering
passed down—
through generations.

to awaken
my emotional digestion—
and release the poisons
that have gathered
within me.

the currents of time

time is never late,
but it leaves early
when chased.

a watch clings
like a whisper
to your wrist,
but time
threads through bone—
a hum
you didn't know
was yours.

you ride it—
slow,
fast—
as you please.

some
choose the saddle,
others
become the wind.

a bee lingers
over a flower,
remembering a colour
it has never seen—
held aloft
by the memory
of perfume.

an eagle glides
in the hush,
the wide frame of the world
folded in its gaze.

a falcon
is an arrow—
too fast
to see
what passes
beneath its wings.

time isn't something
you can hold,
but you can
let it breathe
in your bones,
like music
playing in your soul.

colour.
sound.
taste.
scent.
touch.

these are not
your senses—
they are
time's windows
you can open.

what runs
through your thoughts,
the silence
slipping through your soul,
and the whispers
murmuring in your heart,
are the currents
of your time.

not the watch
on your wrist,
not the clock
on your wall.

words that waited

I never understood
what loving me meant to you—
how your heart lifted
at the jingle of my keys,
how each pause in the hallway
became a prayer
held between breath and wood,
until it ended
in my voice.

I didn't know
how sleep slipped from your shoulders
when I stayed away—
how love becomes a vigil,
a quiet lamp in the window,
still burning
long after the house
faded into dark.

I couldn't see
what your eyes carried
when they met mine—
how your joy
was never joy alone,
but a quiet surrender—
the kind
that holds a whole world
and asks nothing in return.

forgive me
for the quickness of my judgments—
for not asking
what grief you folded
into the creases of your smile,
what hunger you swallowed
so I could eat first
from the plate of life.

forgive me
for not standing beside you
when your legs ached
from carrying the weight
of my silences—
while you stood,
day after day,
cradling the warmth
of a memory—
like a photograph
held too long in the dark,
its corners curled
by longing.

I hope
the echoes were enough—
the laughter of my boyhood
rising like sunlight
on your tired chest,
a whole season
living only in your arms.

I know
I failed in ways
you never named—
but believe me,
I tried—
not to become
what you imagined,
but to be
the man
who might one day
deserve your love.

I had to leave
to learn
who I was—
and even that
I did clumsily.

you taught me
kindness that walks
without sound,
truth that glows
without spectacle—
you placed invisible tools
in my hands,
then turned away,
as if love
were something
to be given,
never claimed.

no one
has loved me
with the patience
you did—
and I
have yet to love
as selflessly.
that's the sorrow
that stays.

I write these
words that waited—
too long, perhaps—
but they are yours.

forgive
this slow blooming—
this long road
back to you.
I carried my own shadows,
fought quiet wars
beneath my skin,
and lost names
I once believed were mine.

still—
you were my first
and fiercest sky.
and now—
if this letter finds you
anywhere at all,
may it sound like the boy

you once rocked
to sleep—
and may it smell
like spring
before it has a name.

what survives

not everything
can be healed—
or held back—
like rot
in the roots
of a hollow tree,
like the hush
around a dying pup,
like the slow undoing
of touch
where love once lived.

you learn
to wear absence
like a second skin—
quiet,
but unbroken.

you survive
not by mending,
but by becoming
the wound
that sings.

longing's threads

desire
is not a trespass—

it is the pulse
beneath stone,
the glint
in gravity's grin.

pleasure—
a lens
the cosmos lifts
to its own skin,
aching
to be seen.

we are
the curve
it leans through,
to feel
its spark
flare
into form.

even your silence has ancestors

not all weight
was chosen—

some entered before breath,
like rain into seed,
like the hush of a mother's hunger
passed through milk.

you came
not as a single note,
but an echo
of everything before you—

the lands your feet never touched,
the hands that fed your parents,
the droughts your name cannot remember
but still thirsts for.

even your silence
has ancestors.

some threads twist from ash,
others from honey—
but all are needed
to hold the shape
you didn't ask for
but became.

if the path bends strangely,
it may be carrying
someone else's fall.

if the light wavers,
perhaps it flickers
through a fabric
not entirely yours.

this is not failure.

you are not the architect
of every storm
you sleep inside.

some winds
blew through
long before your windows
knew glass.

so—
when you feel uneven,
don't sharpen the edges.

undo gently
what can be undone.
love what can't.

walk toward yourself
as if approaching
a child who never
once
meant
harm.

you are allowed
to be tender
with the ones
you once were.

that softness
is not surrender—
it is how imbalance
begins to heal.

a puzzle with no frame

when you take
a piece of soft clay
and press it
into your own shape—
you haven't
met the truth—

truth is layered,
its outlines
blurred or hidden,
a shifting skin
with infinite angles
for the eye
to misplace
or conjure.

and what about
the light
you carry
in your eyes?

you've only
translated it,
bent it
to suit your gaze—
nothing less,
nothing more.

you see
what you need to see—

something to comfort,
something to close
the question
you couldn't bear—
a puzzle
with no frame,
with no face.

let others
have their own shapes,
their own strange selves—
truth is not
a thing you can touch,
not a form
you can mold.

salt does not mourn

I can carry sorrow.
even when it leaks
through my ribs like thaw.

I can hold rage
long enough
to burn it down
to breathe.

what breaks me
is when sorrow
slips its face—
becomes fire
in the throat
of rain.

a river that no longer
knows its water.

a petal
floating too long
to remember
it never belonged.

this is how the ache
for softness
becomes something
with teeth.

how the need to be seen
turns into smoke
that bites the eye
that begged for light.

you ask
why I wince
at kindness—
it's because I've learned
how salt
can come
draped in a kiss.

and salt
does not mourn
what it ruins.

neither black, nor white

maybe
there is no black—
no white.

maybe right
and wrong
are just shadows cast
by where you're standing
when the light bends.

what if truth
isn't a sword,
but a mirror—
and every face
leaves a different
fog on the glass?

pause.
don't try
to convince the sky
which shape a cloud should take.

let others be.
let yourself be.
even the wind
has no need
to be right.

the lie that sees me

who am I lying to?
do I want to be liked,
respected,
loved—
or simply
to be believed?

or am I afraid
of knowing
who I am
when no one's watching?

maybe I've built a face
that smiles too easily—
a shape easier to wear
through rooms
that never ask
what's beneath.

is it really for them—
or have I been
gently
teaching myself
to love
the reflection
they approve of?

truth has no mirrors,
and I've only learned
to love
what reflects.

so who am I lying to?

maybe the lie
was just a candle
lit in a cold hallway—
a way to see my own hands,
to feel
like I am still here.

but there is a room
I haven't opened—
a quiet heart
no one has stepped into
to light
even a little of it.

ànd I wait,
half-ashamed,
half-hoping
that someone might still come
and strike
a single match.

flicker beneath

some are stitched
from louder absences—
hollows that breathe
like mouths
sewn into the wind.

others—
barely remembered
even by their own shadows,
as if erased
before being drawn.

but all of us
carry a thirst
to be held
in someone's seeing—
not as a shape—
but as the flicker beneath it,
like light
forgetting its name
inside a body.

perhaps
this ache
is only the echo
of how unevenly
the soul was watered—

one soul fed
from clouds
that whispered in sleep,

the other
left beneath a sky
that swallowed its rain—
then stitched silence back.

the shape of pleasure

pleasure
is not the spark—
but the pattern
left in the ash.

it arrives
layered,
like rain falling
through skin, heart, thought,
and the soul's sky.

not a flash,
but a folding—
existence
learning to echo
its own touch.

just like life,
it unveils itself
not all at once—
but in waves
that remember
what it means
to feel
alive.

the hollow deal

is it a crime—
or the greatest sin—
to hijack love
and wear it
like a borrowed skin?

or is it hunger,
pale and thin,
gnawing the soul
from a hollow
within?

the hole inside—
how deep it runs,
a well with no bottom,
no moon,
no sun.

each kiss becomes
another deal,
another mask,
another peel.
yet the hunger
doesn't heal,
the void too raw
to ever seal.

yes—
a silent theft,
a quiet war
on what is left.

to take a heartbeat,
soft and whole,
and carve it open
just to fill
a hole.

carved from the dark

is it hate
that shaped your heart
into stone,
or did a heart of stone
give birth
to hatred?

was the heart
born sealed—
or buried
so deep,
so dark,
it mistook pressure
for love
and became rock?

or maybe
sometimes—
they carve one another
from the same dark.

where no one dwells

you don't have to
believe in anything.

but when you stop
believing in those
who love you—
or at least
still lean toward your name
like grass toward light—

you begin to carve
an open wound
where a river once remembered
its way to your chest.

before long,
before you even look back,
the valley of you
is wind-scoured,
weathered into
a desert that forgets
how to bloom.

no petals.
no pulse.
no water
for the thirst you won't name.

no bird
with a sky to borrow.

no voice
to cradle your ache.

a ruin,
so forsaken,
even you
refuse to dwell there.

you don't just
push the world away—
you vanish
from the threshold
of your own soul.

above the path

somewhere—
darker than pain,
heavier than sorrow—
you walk.

and you fall.
your knees
have forgotten
how to speak.

but above you,
something
with wings
remembers your name—
and flies.

it watches
how silence takes shape
as it leans
against the wind.

it does not cry—
it circles.
it does not leave—
it sings.

and waits
for your shadow
to lift its face.

there is a part of you
that remains whole—
just enough
to carry what's broken.

that is the flight.
that is the warmth
returning to your hands
like the light
you forgot
was yours.

and now—
you rise.
not because it ends,
but because
it remembers you.

when it arrives

it doesn't knock—
it enters
along your spine,
like light
slipping into a well
that forgot it was deep.

you do not think.
you dissolve—
a mouth
becoming river,
a hand
remembering
how to speak
without words.

poetry
is not written.
it blooms
between the ribs,
then walks out
on your breath
like it knows
why it was born.

sometimes
you say something
and the air around you
leans in,
as if the world
just remembered

it once had
an ear
for listening.

this is the moment
you are most yourself—
not because you meant to,
but because
you disappeared
in exactly the right way.

hunger for hunger

it's painted
not for your eyes—
but your thirst.

not to be reached,
only to remain
barely out of ache.

not a trick,
but an agreement
between longing
and the shape it takes
to stay unheld.

it learns you
more intimately
than you've ever been named—
knows how to shimmer
where your map begins to tear.

you walk
because there's something
just ahead
that keeps not happening.

and in not happening,
it becomes a season
you chase.

you forget
what you were seeking
until the seeking
becomes
its own kind of hunger.

eventually,
you stop asking
if it's real.

you don't want
to find it anymore—
only to need
the never-finding.

a breath of eternity

why does the poet always reach
for the rose—
beauty, grace,
a staged pose,
a scent that vanishes
as it blooms?

why not the scent
of my dog,
curled against me—
a quiet sun
melting into my pillow,
warming night's bones,
filling the dark
with a river
of soft, wordless love?

why not his nose—
that soft, wet, curious key
unseaming
the folds of reality?

why not the quiet purity
in the brown galaxies of his eyes,
a gift from a time
not merely ancient,
but formed
from the memory of stardust
before form,
before time folded into history,
before Cyrus etched

his dreams of justice
into clay?

why not his silence—
a song of weightless bones,
a language
where touch is sound,
and every glance
a prayer to the unseen?

why not the joy
that erupts when I return—
his tail a pendulum
between worlds,
the room blooming
with light that has no source?

why not that grateful tongue,
scribbling constellations
across my skin,
lifting life
into a dimension
where gravity forgets its name
and love drips like honey
through the cracks in the real?

why not his unknowing—
a grace untouched
by mirrors,
by the ticking of clocks,
by the cold whisper of endings?

he doesn't know
he'll vanish.
but I do.

still, he gives—
his breath,
his warmth,
his quiet weight
against my chest.

and when he goes,
he will remain—
scattered
through the corridors
of my bones,
glowing softly
in the dark.

a breath of eternity—
unlost,
unending.

no diagrams for wind

you never mapped
how salt enters bread,
or why
the wing tilts
just before sky agrees.

but you ate.
you flew.

the root doesn't theorise water—
it drinks.
the flame doesn't explain longing—
it leans.

whatever life is,
it arrives unmarked,
like a language
the body remembers
only after the speaking has passed.

and you—
a chord struck by no hand—
still trembling
only because the world
was quiet enough
to let you happen.

the last warmth

I could dissolve
if thrown
into a flame—
a breathless ember
drifting through dusk.

I could grow lungs
beneath the ice,
instruct my blood
to quiet its weather
within the drowning's hush.

yet I
cannot loosen
the smallest thread
of you.

I cannot
set down
a love
so gentle
it moves across
the air
like a presence
that was never light enough
to be seen.

I just can't
step
where your name
does not follow.

the final kiss—
a silence
with no skin—
burning inward,
never thawing.

breath of mist

whether I have a soul or not,
there is something
within me
that rises above me—
gently,
and dances,
warms the cold air
around me,
floats weightlessly,
and in time
ascends
to join the clouds,
just like a breath of mist.

when I keep
some warmth
in my heart,
and in my bones,
and every vein,
and every cell
that forms
who I am,
it rises,
it dances,
it floats,
and it ascends,
to reach the land
that needs it most.

and if I don't—
it doesn't.

threads of the whole

nothing arrives alone—
the current signs in both directions
and every silence
leans against a sound
it does not interrupt.

a stone does not ask
why it is shaped by both
weight and wind.
it simply becomes
what cannot be unmade.

within the atom,
a pulse moves forward
by moving against—
not war,
but weave.

light needs
its dim to mean,
as breath needs
its hollow
to echo.

the world does not divide—
it folds,
like flame curving
only by holding
its own extinction.

to live
is not to choose
but to sift,
like roots learning
what to keep
without naming waste.

and you,
a brief resonance
within this symmetry—
not to escape it,
but to move
with what moves everything.

let me hear the sky you carry

now I know—
joy is not a thing to be kept,
but a light that shivers
until it finds another skin,
trembling into warmth.

when I speak of moments
that made my heart ring
like a spoon tapped
against the rim of time,
it is not for the telling—
but for the weaving:
a thread cast slowly
from my breath
to yours.

I want you to know
what the sun felt like
when it landed on my shoulder—
as if it had chosen me
from a million spines.

I want you to know
how laughter once spilled
from a stranger's silence
and gathered in my hands
like rain astonished to find it was water.

these are not stories.
these are soft translations
of the love I carry

toward the constellation
that is you.

so let me listen
to the sky you carry
inside your ribs.

let me hold the fragments
of your unseen mornings—
the inkblot memories,
the almost-heard songs
you thought had no place to go.

do not silence the winds
that speak your name
in languages more ancient than breath.

do not deny me the gift
of disappearing into your voice
the way rivers forget themselves
not at the sea—
but in the moment surrender begins.

a crown of forgetting

do you believe
you know more
than a bee?

is knowledge
just what survives
your gaze—
or only
what bends
to the shape
of your questions?

you name it seeing—
but is it seeing,
or just forgetting
everything
that doesn't
echo your shape?

if you can't feel
what the bee knows,
it doesn't mean
you know more—
only that your knowing
has grown
too stiff to rise.

you define wisdom
as a shape
you can sit in.
the bee

slips through it—
like wind between
your fingers.

do you think
you're kinder
than the fungus
breathing beneath
your boots?

its filaments
weave soil
into song,
mending
what you break—
not once asking
to be seen.

you crown yourself:
lion of land,
eagle of sky,
leviathan
of the sea—
each throne
made from a mirror
that forgets
it once was sand.

you act
like the god
you invented—
a snowball
rolling downhill,

hoarding names,
forgetting the edge.

you move
like an heir
to a wound
you've never seen.

but tell me—
do you know more
than the bee—
the ancient
geometer
of nectar's cathedral,
the pulse
beneath the fruit
you swallow?

colours have no name

when you name it,
a door closes—
not loudly,
but like mist
leaving a field
at dawn.

a shape appears,
and something vanishes.
the outline holds—
but the breath
has gone.

it holds,
like a jar
holds water—
never the river,
never the rain.

there is a joy
the tongue forgets—
a silence
the eye remembers
from before
it could name
what it saw.

the first eyes
did not speak—
they opened,
and that was enough.

a flower
was once a gesture,
not a word.
a scent,
not a sentence.

you think
to name
is to know—
but knowing
isn't always
what truth asks for.

say, *blue*,
and something
falls away—
what lived
between
blue and *not-blue*.

what we call colour
is only the body
light wears
in our presence.
the rest—
it saves
for silence.

we see so little:
a sliver of spectrum,
a whisper
of what light

remembers.

and still
we carve the world
into pieces
we can pronounce,
never noticing
how much escapes
each time.

there is a kind of love
in not naming.
a kind of wisdom
in letting things be.

perhaps
the truest understanding
is not what you can hold,
but what you are
willing to stand before—
unarmed.

and maybe heaven
isn't a place
but a way of seeing,
a way of being—
where colour has no name
and nothing longs for one.

connect with the author

Thank you for reading. If the work moved you, I would be grateful if you shared your thoughts by leaving a review on Amazon.

LinkTree Website for all links
https://linktr.ee/andrepbpoetry

andre pb poetry website

linktr.ee/andrepbpoetry

Instagram
@andrepbpoetry
https://www.instagram.com/andrepbpoetry/

Email
andre.pb.poetry@gmail.com

www.ingramcontent.com/pod-product-compliance
Lightning Source LLC
Chambersburg PA
CBHW031538040426
42445CB00010B/600